The Exodus Road

Laura Parker

with Matt Parker

Contents

Dear Reader,

If you told me when I married my high school sweetheart, at just barely 21, that I would eventually send him into brothels in SouthEast Asia, I would have said you're crazy.

If you told me that my youth pastor husband would one day be wearing undercover surveillance gear and entering hotel lobbies run by the Russian mafia, I would have said you had picked the wrong girl, the wrong marriage, the wrong career.

If you hinted on my wedding day as I wore white that 13 years later I would regularly watch my husband ask for sex from young girls via his covert footage, from our home in Malaysia with three sleeping children upstairs, there's no way I would've believed you.

And maybe I would have reconsidered walking the aisle in the first place.

But we don't get to choose the future, often don't get to write our own stories. Our "yes" at an altar is an act of faith because we don't know what we're signing up for — not *really*. Sometimes there are dark and brutal bends in the road, twists impossible to imagine.

This book is our story of those gritty places; it's the tale of the brothels we never expected to find ourselves in. It's a story that doesn't involve a Jason Bourne, Mother Teresa or superhero. It's a story, instead, of failure, fear, isolation and the very, *very* ordinary.

And it's a story, to us, at least, of rescue — both for children trapped in sexual slavery and for ourselves, caught in the assumption that human trafficking was a problem which *other* people should help solve.

My hope in the telling of our journey is that you might see the bitter realities of the oppressed and become inspired to rise up to fight on their behalf--

even though you may very well be as ordinary as we are.

For Rescue,

Laura Parker
July 2013

LauraParkerWrites.com | TheExodusRoad.com

Disclaimers

A Humble Admission. There are many more qualified people than Matt or Laura Parker to talk about the issues surrounding human trafficking. We have been honored to meet scores of educated, experienced, and dedicated individuals who have logged *years* in freedom efforts before we even set foot on Asian soil. To these people, we remain indebted and inspired.

More specifically, we are humbled to have had the opportunity to work with brave investigators on the ground, many of whom also have leagues more experience than ourselves. While we were able to get our toes in shallow water for nine months in roughly 250 brothels, we respect the men (and women) who have fought for others' rescue from the deep end for decades. These are the true heroes.

For Security Measures: Names, dates, places and some details have been changed to protect the privacy and security of those involved in undercover work. We describe events as accurately as possible, but some liberties have been taken in an effort to tell a more engaging story. Experiences and cases, while all true, have been rearranged to better fit our storytelling — especially the sections given from a wife's perspective.

A Note About Faith: The Exodus Road is not a Christian organization. Our coalition supports Muslims, Buddhists, Atheists, Hindus and others of varying faith and political backgrounds. We are committed to rallying many around justice for the modern-day slave, regardless of religious beliefs or political leanings. However, since this book is a recording of our *personal* story as founders, we do write from a Christian perspective. To neglect the faith piece of our own story would feel grossly inauthentic, as trying to follow the way of Jesus remains the single greatest motivator for our lives.

Investigative Practices: The journey recorded in the following pages does not relay best investigative practices by any means. Our own understanding of effective investigations has grown greatly since Matt ventured out on his first mission and is still developing today as we collaborate with trained investigators around the world. Honestly, much of that first year would fall more into the category of "research and development."

Prostitution vs. Trafficking: It's important to understand the difference between those choosing to engage in prostitution as an employment option and those who classify as trafficked victims. Men, women, and children who are trafficked do not have the ability to walk away from their pimps or brokers because of force, debt, violence, fraud, or coercion (see the *UN* definition of *human trafficking* in the following section). While we would agree that there is often exploitation in prostitution itself, the work described in these pages is not primarily centered around "rescuing" or ministering to prostitutes—though this is noble, important work. Rather, our efforts are focused on gaining freedom from sex trafficking for those who are trapped against their wills or who work in the sex trade and are under the age of 18 years old.

A Final Statement: Though this book depicts our own path into undercover investigations with sexual slavery, we recognize this is an extremely dangerous world on many fronts— physically, morally and spiritually. We are *not* in any way advocating that untrained men and women, without support or accountability, strap on covert cameras and charge into brothels.

There.

We just felt we needed to say that.

The Facts of

Modern-Day Slavery

"Slavery occurs when one person completely controls another person, using violence or the threat of violence to maintain that control, exploits them economically, pays them nothing and they cannot walk away."

CNN Freedom Project

"Trafficking in Persons is the recruitment, transportation, transfer, harboring, or receipt of person by means of threat or use of force or other forms of coercion, of abduction, of fraud, of deception, or the abuse of power . . . for the purpose of exploitation.

Exploitation shall include. . . prostitution of other or other forms of sexual exploitation, forced labor or service, slavery or practices similar to slavery, servitude or the removal of organs."

The United Nations

There are an estimated 10-30 million modern day slaves today, more than at any other time in human history. The majority of slavery occurs in Asian and African countries.

An average slave in the American South in 1850 cost the
equivalent of $40,000 in today's money; today a slave costs an
average of $90.

Free the Slaves

Human trafficking is the third largest international criminal
business, grossing an estimated 32 billion USD each year.

UN Office on Drugs and Crime

Trafficking occurs in 161 of the 195 countries. Of the modern-
day slaves, an estimated 70% are women and up to 50% are
children.

CNN Freedom Project

Between 14,500 – 17,500 new slaves are brought into the United
States every year across international borders.

US Department of State

It is estimated that 21% of all forced labor in the global sex
industry is comprised of children.

International Labor Organization

"We worked six days a week and twelve hours a day. We mostly
had to serve 32-35 clients a day . . . If anyone refused to be with
a customer, we were beaten. If we adamantly refused, the pimps
would show us a lesson by raping us."

"Maria," 17 Year Old Sex Trafficking Survivor, Polaris Project

Preface

Crumbs and Minnows

"With the possible exception of the equator, everything begins somewhere."
- C.S. Lewis

"Bring what you have."
- Jesus

I looked beyond my husband's back and saw faces of the people I loved. From the church stage, I scanned the familiar crowd. Women who had brought me meals with both miscarriage and birth. Friends who sat around campfires, sipped wine and talked of things that mattered. Mothers who became like sisters over hours spent in playdates at the park.

This was my community. My people, my tribe.

And we were leaving it.

I felt tears well and told myself to keep it together. No one wants to see a missionary fall apart on stage two weeks before the boat shoves off.

Yet, I knew this move was right, was good. Through a series of events and the stirring of spirit, we had made the decision to leave the church my husband, Matt, had served for the past four years in Colorado. We were moving our family of five overseas to Kota Baharu, Malaysia, to direct a Children's Home for impoverished girls from the hill tribes of the region.

The plane left in 8 days. And we had no idea when we'd be back.

The tears pricked again.

My husband's voice broke through scattered thoughts. He told the Sunday crowd his favorite story of Jesus and a multitude of hungry people.

Jesus had been on a hill talking to a huge crowd all day. As dinnertime neared, his friends approached the rabbi and said there were too many mouths to feed, that the masses should be sent away. And Jesus looked at these motley twelve and spoke the unexpected, *"You* feed them. Bring what you have."

The disciples scrambled and found five loaves and two fish — a woefully inadequate provision for such a colossal need.

But Jesus took what they offered—pitiful lunch that it was —broke it, blessed it, and met the needs of the masses.

A miracle with the ordinary.

❈ ❈ ❈ ❈ ❈

Two months later, I threw my bike across the front yard and cussed up a storm. I was trying to get to language school across town which required four different forms of transportation, and a flat tire in the tropical heat had made me miss the first bus.

Things were not going well here in Malaysia.

The next 10 months were no better. My five year old son Owen packed his bag and demanded to go home. We faced conflict and confrontation in our new job from Day Three. We battled rats in our kitchen and a language that literally sounded like make-believe. I was too afraid to drive, and Matt was too culture-shocked to laugh. Poverty and injustice assaulted us at every marketplace and on every street corner. Our family was in crisis.

We stayed in the thick of it for an entire year, until, mercifully, the air began to clear.

We trained a local Malaysian to direct the Children's Home we'd been working at, and we were able to step out of that original job role which had proven all-consuming.

We took our first family vacation to the beach, an exotic one at that, underlining the fact that living overseas could have its perks. And soon after, we moved out of rural Malaysia and into the city which provided more modern conveniences.

Through tutors and time, we gained a basic grasp of the language and the culture, and I eventually learned to drive both a motorbike and a car on the left side of the road.

And while we were unaware of the darkness we would step into and the fears we would face in the coming months, we had learned something incredibly valuable from that first brutal year overseas. Unlike ever before, we had grown intimately acquainted with our shortcomings, our failures, our crutches. We'd learned through tears and mistakes and tantrums that we weren't even able to bring five loaves and two fish to the needs around us.

All we could muster was a few crumbs and a couple of minnows.

We hoped it would be enough.

Chapter One

Wild Dogs

"This is your last chance. After this, there is no turning back. You take the blue pill—the story ends, you wake up in your bed and you believe . . . whatever you want to believe. You take the red pill—you stay . . . And I show you how deep the rabbit hole goes."

- The Matrix

Rice again for dinner.

I emptied a red curry I'd bought at the local market into a bowl. I'd piled three kids and myself on a motorbike earlier that night, and we'd navigated around squirming eels in buckets and throngs of hard-working Malaysians to purchase supper. Back in my kitchen, I tore open a bag of fresh pineapple I'd bought to compliment the curry, and I ignored a twinge of anxiety. I'd read warning after warning about the dangers of local fruit prepared with gloveless hands in unsanitary conditions, but time spent on foreign soil forces a mother to choose her battles. Funny how absolute convenience can win out over chance nausea.

I squirted ketchup on paper plates in front of me while I

checked the phone for texts. Ketchup was a luxury saved for Western pizza in this part of the world, but my two youngest wouldn't eat rice without it. Over the past months, I'd tried bribes and I'd tried the "fine, just go hungry" tactic, but to no avail. I always caved. We yanked the kids from all they'd ever known and stuck them in a third world country, after all. Call it guilt-induced-parenting, but I finally succumbed to lifting ketchup packets from McDonald's and stashing the condiment-treasures in a plastic bag in my purse.

I reckon even missionaries can steal.

Ding. A message from my husband. I looked at the green text box on my phone.

Matt: Praying with the guys now. Probably head out in an hour.

"Is that Dad?" my eight year old daughter Tess asked, more perceptive than a counselor of twenty years. At the expense of our privacy, she was analyzing us better each day.

I slipped the phone off the table and into my back pocket.

"Yeah, he's fine. Having a good time with his friends," I answered. I rationalized the statement with the fact that the two men he was with were, actually, our real-life friends, even though I knew the three had not signed up for a relaxing weekend away.

I didn't want to tell my innocent daughter that her daddy

was about to step into one of the darkest places of his life.

Apparently, missionaries can lie, too.

❀ ❀ ❀ ❀

The tropic-heat finally faded by 7 p.m., so I herded children outside to ride bikes around the neighborhood. We lived in a gated community in the city, nicer by far than the previous two places we'd lived in a rural village outside of Kota Baharu. And despite my "live-like-the-natives" idealism, I'd seen the wild dogs in most local neighborhoods without the guards and the gates. They were mangy, skinny and desperate, and I'd quickly learned that compassion for neglected animals is a luxury mothers with small children cannot afford in developing countries.

In fact, several months earlier, two street dogs had snarled and lunged for Matt, causing him to wreck his motorcycle, pride, and new suit pants. He had bloodied both knees and threw out his back on a busy city street with those angry animals still barking. That experience, along with the threat of the *nine* rabies shots awaiting any unlucky victim after a bite, and we'd learned that protection from wild dogs was worth the monthly investment into neighborhood gates and the guards that stood at them.

Wild dogs are wild dogs, after all. Neglected, sadly. But dangerous? *Absolutely.*

Three year old Lilly climbed onto the back seat of my tall red bike with its upright handlebars. The basket up front reminded me of *The Wizard of Oz*, though I kept hoping my kids would see more Dorothy in me than Wicked Witch of the West.

Ding. Another incoming text. I fished the phone out of pocket.

Matt: Hope you're having fun. Miss you and the kids. Nervous, but feeling like it is right. You still okay with this?

I straddled the bike and the 30-pound child on the back and typed while calling ahead for my son to wait for me, *Yes. Praying. Gotta go. Love you.*

We began our usual path around the neighborhood while my mind raced down new territory unfolding several hundred miles away. *What are we thinking? We've been* proud *of never going into these places before.*

I pedaled. Questions churned.

What if he gets hurt? What will he see and what if he likes what he sees? And isn't this whole thing way worse than porn?

❈ ❈ ❈ ❈ ❈

Ding.

Matt: We're here. About to go in. I'm nervous.

"Owen, the hot water's out again. But, yes, you still have to shower. Lilly, brush your teeth. Tess, did you feed the cat?"

Ding.

Matt: Talking to owner at Pink Lady. Having a drink. No girls yet.

"If you don't get in your bed by the count of three. . . ." I wrestled dirty clothes into hampers and kids under covers. It was a long half-hour past bedtimes, and they still hadn't picked up their rooms.

Ding.

Matt: Sitting with a 15-year-old. Her name is Mahi.

"Jesus, bless Tess, Owen, and Lilly while they sleep, help them to know they are loved and safe in your arms." I kissed foreheads and delivered pink blankets. One more trip downstairs to get water.

Ding.

Matt: In the bathroom. Needed a break. This is harder than I thought.

❀ ❀ ❀ ❀ ❀

And it was harder than I thought, too. This straddling of two worlds, the sheltering of one from the other. It was like I was on foot in a back alley with a pack of snarling wild dogs closing in.

And the gates and the guards that shielded our innocence were no more.

Knocked down and thrown open by our very own hands.

Chapter Two

Backs that Bend

"Change does not roll in on wheels of inevitability, but
comes through continuous struggle. And so we
must straighten our backs
and work for . . . freedom."
- Martin Luther King, Jr.

"All the commandments are summed
up in this single command:
You must love your neighbor as yourself."
- Jesus

I handed over a cup of coffee—the instant kind we'd gotten
used to. Enough cream and sugar could make anything decent.
And while the coffee wasn't gourmet, the view was a feast.
From our second floor balcony, we could see a rice field spread
beyond our whitewashed wall. On the other side, a small village
of people lived, in both shacks and deeper community than I'd
ever known.

The kids lounged downstairs watching another episode of

Little House on the Prairie. We were up to the fourth season now, and we all still hated Nellie.

"So, tell me. Tell me it all," I said to my drowsy husband, unsure if I really wanted the full-monty version. He'd been sleeping since the plane landed six hours ago.

He began—this man who was always pushing envelopes. And he told me in the straight honesty I admired about him— told me *everything*.

He talked about the 15 year old, Mahi, who sat with him most of the first night, and he told me how girls stood on stage with numbers pinned to the shoulder straps of their short dresses.

"How do you pick which one comes off stage and sits beside you?" he asked in a voice barely a whisper. This from the man who both cried at Hallmark commercials and fought-like-mad against any form of injustice. His hazel eyes were on the rice field, and he knew I didn't have an answer. He was shell-shocked and quiet, visibly tormented and broken.

I glanced at the Malaysian farmer bent over his rice plants on the other side of our wall. Mud boots nearly reached his knees as he stood in a flooded field. He bent over to place small sprouts of rice in the water-soaked earth. And I wondered how his back wasn't killing him. Mine hurt with carrying and birthing babies—a process that lasted a few months. His was bent all day, most days.

Perhaps there's a greater resistance and numbing to pain when the stress is constant, rather than brought on unexpected-like.

✻ ✻ ✻ ✻ ✻

One week earlier, Matt's phone rang with a call from a contact who worked in the nearby city of Kangar. This woman spent time developing relationships with prostitutes and offering them alternative job solutions, and she'd recently seen something unsettling. She told Matt of a suspicious bar in their city which, under the guise of an orphanage, had pictures of young girls taped to the back wall. The aid worker asked if Matt knew of anyone who would go into the bar and ask questions—pose as a "john" and find out if there were children for sale for sex. Despite making 12 phone calls to organizations specifically working in counter-trafficking in the area, he found no one willing or able to go.

Finally, two of his friends, inexperienced but desiring to help, agreed to take the assignment.

But, then, the curve ball.

They asked Matt to come, too.

A youth pastor, a businessman, and a former missionary-kid formed the team on that first investigative operation. None of them had ever visited a strip club before. None had undercover or military experience. The unlikely group was comprised of three ordinary men with kids and wives and their favorite football teams. They had each moved their families halfway around the world to fight slavery and felt that the photos on the back wall were worth investigating. They chose action on behalf of a child.

"If you fight a battle, you should expect to get blood-spattered and dirty," one of them said. And so they had boarded buses and stepped into brothels.

❀ ❀ ❀ ❀ ❀

And the farmer planted in the rice field, while I harvested answers on the porch. I asked for all of the weekend's details that morning. And he gave them to me. Stories of girls with real names, of overweight men groping teenagers, of strip club after strip club. He pulled out his phone and showed me a picture of Mahi. He had his arm around her and there were bikini-clad women in the background. They were smiling into the photo—my husband and this other girl—but oddly, I wasn't jealous, just deeply sad. Mahi reminded me of the bright-eyed teenagers I'd spent the last ten years mentoring, reminded me of my own beautiful daughters a decade from now.

And we cried. Both of us, for a while, holding bad coffee now cold.

And I looked over the wall at the bent farmer finishing the

first of 12 hours of manual labor that day. I wondered if he knew what was happening to his country's daughters and wondered why he wasn't crying about it like we were.

I suspected he'd always known. His back had been bent his entire life, as had generations before him, after all.

Chapter Three

The Question of the Rock

"In any moment of decision, the best thing you can do is the right thing. The worst thing you can do is nothing."
- Theodore Roosevelt

"If you can't feed a hundred people, then feed just one."
- Mother Teresa

Five people. One scooter.

It quickly became our family's chosen transportation to places close-by—across the street to the *7-11* for bread or a *Coke Zero,* around the neighborhood to the noodle stand, down the back alley to the coffee shop. Scooters in Asia are convenient and cheap, and we'd seen about everything imaginable balanced on them—a television set, a dog, a nursing baby, a ten gallon fish tank.

Matt drove the motorbike while Lilly, the smallest, stood in front of him. With a four-person pileup behind her, she gripped the mirrors on either side of the handlebars. I dangled precariously off the back end of the bike.

Our friends had tipped us off to a hidden coffee shop in the jungle — Garden House, the locals called it. We motored off on a family adventure one Saturday afternoon to find it.

We wove into tropical jungle on roads that alternated between dirt and pavement. The trees and foliage crawled everywhere, thick and green, providing only glimpses of the cinderblock homes common in our part of Malaysia. Tess's blonde hair blew in my face, and Owen's body pressed tight against his father's back. Lilly balanced up front singing songs with made-up words. It was magical. One of those moments as a mother you want to grab and freeze and then pull out to savor in coming years.

And we found it, the Garden House. A creek ran through the center, hanging baskets swayed from the beams of an open air oasis. Beauty cultivated in every space here — from the bamboo furniture on the deck, to the herb garden out front, to the live orchids grafted into the trunks of the trees.

We ordered iced coffees and ice cream and let the kids hunt crawdads in the creek.

I watched them play, these three precious people I've been given to mother. Lilly dropped a rock and created a splash. She laughed loudly, as free-spirits tend to do. Owen tried to get a tiny crustacean to grab a stick, his bright blue eyes focused. Tess coaxed baby fish into the plastic water cup she took from the table. They were happy. They were innocent. They were children.

My. Children.

And Matt and I, we sat and processed the last weekend, that first mission. The value of it; the intel gathered, the emotional fallout. And we asked ourselves the question we'd battled all week: *If a need arose, would we send him out again?*

Matt had spent the previous four months serving on an intervention committee within the NGO (Non Government Organization) community. Even though they had built policies for victim rescue and relationships with local Malaysian police, he had been shocked to find out how very little was being done to actually find and rescue victims of sexual slavery. Though our Google searches about trafficking prior to moving to Malaysia led us to believe that NGO machines were well-oiled in the fight for freedom, our on-the-ground experience had painted a much bleaker picture.

We were finding that in our region the government had woefully inadequate funding or staffing to make a significant dent in the problem, and that the NGO community (especially the faith-based one) was either scared, underfunded, unaware, or unwilling to practically engage in rescue. The process to find victims, document evidence, work with local police, and help physically free a child trapped in sexual abuse took heavy doses of both grit and resources.

Rocks splashed in the creek beside us, dropped by small hands that had been full of baby dolls a few hours before.

Matt watched her too, this youngest of ours.

"What if it were Lilly? If it were Owen? Tess? Wouldn't we want someone to figure it out? Wouldn't we want people to go looking for them, if it were our child's picture taped to the back wall?" It was a question that had weighed heavy for the past week.

Lilly walked up with a rock, a stone that looked like every other rock in the stream bed—dripping wet from its recent home.

"Look what I found!" she exclaimed, a preschool geologist discovering treasure. "It's a *special* rock. Mom, you have to keep it, okay?" And then the emphatic command, *"Don't* lose it."

My daughter saw the rock that day. Blue eyes noticed and valued a treasure forgotten by the wide-world. Little fingers plucked the stone out from the others, lifted it from the mud, and wanted someone else to take notice and care for it, too. And she asked *me* to help.

It was just an ordinary rock from a stream.

But, to me, it was more.

I locked eyes with my husband.

"I think you should go out this week."

Chapter Four

The Floating Door

"No one ever overcomes difficulties by going at them in a
hesitant, doubtful way."
- Laura Ingalls Wilder

"God is in the slums, in the cardboard boxes where the
poor play house. God is in the silence of a mother who has
infected her child with a virus that will end both their lives. God
is in the cries heard under the rubble of war. God is in the
debris of wasted opportunity and lives, and God is with us if
we are with them."
- Bono, *U2*

It was 9 p.m., and though I should have been tired,
adrenaline had kicked in.

Tonight Matt was going out again.

This time, alone.

The idea was to ask a *tuk-tuk* (motorcycle taxi) driver for
young girls and see where he led. The plan made both of us

nervous and would have been far better if it involved backup—a partner to go with Matt or to at least track him remotely.

But we'd already asked everyone we knew and had found no takers.

"You shouldn't be doing this by yourself," we'd heard from friends, missionaries, humanitarian workers.

"Then come with me," Matt had said to each.

"No, no I couldn't do that," was the usual reply.

And we got it, we did. There are a million reasons why upstanding moral men don't belong in strip clubs. A million. There are marriages, triggers and dangers. There are reputations to protect and pitfalls to avoid. There are entire organizations whose work might crumble if they sanctioned undercover work in brothels.

Yet, *yet.*

We still couldn't get away from this idea that if it were our daughter, we'd want someone to go looking for her, want someone, somewhere, to fight for her rescue—regardless of the red tape or danger.

We couldn't get past the idea that maybe there *was* a noble reason for a good man to frequent a brothel, after all.

❖ ❖ ❖ ❖ ❖

Kids asleep upstairs, and I stared at his hands in mine. We started to pray. These hands that held mine nervously in a movie theater for the first time as seniors in high school. We had gone to see *Titanic* when it first came out on the big screen, and I remember crying through the entire last half as an emotional teenager, watching wild, sacrificial romance unfold. In a sea of ice, Jack, the lead character, had a choice to make as the last lights of the Titanic sank; it was him or her on a single piece of ship wreckage—a floating door—not strong enough to hold them both.

Oh, how I cried for the tragedy of it.

And Matt held my hand through that movie, just like he held it on beaches in Mexico and beside hospital beds welcoming babies. His hand had grabbed mine at weddings and dinner tables and Christmas events for the past 15 years.

And these same hands would be handing over cash to a driver that night.

His scooter lights faded in the distance around the corner, leaving me to my own thoughts and prayers. The laptop lay open and the plan was to Skype-chat throughout the night. I didn't want him to feel alone.

"Maybe he has backup, after all," I thought.

❀ ❀ ❀ ❀ ❀

Ding.

Matt: Getting in tuk-tuk now. Guy says he knows some places.

I listened to the same song on repeat about darkness running from Light.

I journaled and checked Facebook.

Ding.

Matt: At first place, north of city. Young girls, but no one under 18. Going to next place soon.

I got cup of coffee and read Jesus's words about overcoming the world.

It was getting late, nearing 1:30 a.m.

Ding.

Matt: That was hard. Taken to storefront downtown. No idea it was brothel. Girls were asleep on floor. He's taking me one more place.

I felt sick. I Googled homeschooling ideas, because my brain and my spirit had hit a wall. I checked Facebook again.

And again.

I fell asleep around 2:30 a.m. with the laptop open and the volume turned up, so I could hear the next time he texted.

Ding. I lifted groggy eyes to screen.

Matt: Bottom floor of big hotel. Line of girls behind glass with numbers. Maybe under 18. Called a fishbowl. Hard. Spent a lot of $ tonight. Be home in 30 minutes.

I felt heavy, disturbed, but finally drifted off again.

I barely woke up as hands brushed my shoulder.

He smelled like smoke and alcohol and collapsed on top of the covers. Words escaped him tonight, though I knew they would come in the morning.

It was 3:30 a.m., and I grabbed his hand—in a bed of real life, not an icy sea on the big screen. I prayed it wouldn't turn out to be him or me as ship lights sank. I hoped there'd be room enough for *both* of us on the floating door, till morning or rescue, whichever came first.

Chapter Five

Hot Glue Gun

"We are too young to realize that certain
things are impossible . . .
So we will do them anyway."
- William Wilberforce

"But God chose the foolish things of the world to shame
the wise; God chose the weak things to shame the strong."
- Apostle Paul

"Babe, do we have a hot glue gun?"

I was trying to teach my son about silent *e*'s, while telling my daughter, "Yes, you do have to do your best, what kind of question is that?" In the midst of this, I attempted to keep the play dough my preschooler was pounding into pretend snakes off the floor.

Yet another chaotic day homeschooling; one of those days I wished we could afford the international school down the street.

I barely paid attention to the request, but fished the hot glue gun out from under stickers in the art drawer.

"Don't let the kids come upstairs, okay?" he whispered intently and secretly.

Suddenly, hot glue became deeply intriguing.

Ten minutes later, I left the kids with a project and a threat and opened the closed door to our bedroom. I found Matt hunched over the computer bag he'd bought off Amazon three years ago. The thing had literally traveled the world with us, and now he repaid its service by hacking its vinyl and tearing the inside pockets. An *exacto* knife, rolls of velcro, and that hot glue gun had all been called into service.

❄ ❄ ❄ ❄ ❄

Two weeks earlier, Matt had visited the local Malaysian police sergeant in Kota Baharu. This particular sergeant was directly responsible for all human trafficking and sexual slavery cases in the entire northern province of Malaysia, including the border into neighboring Thailand — a known highway for traffickers. The Malaysian native had a team of four men who worked with him, each with only $100 monthly from the government with which to conduct all of their police activities. A pitiful amount, considering Matt had been spending $100 a *night* doing simple ground-level surveillance.

My husband had developed a working relationship with this

sergeant, a man nobly committed to justice in his own country. Matt wanted to make his own role as an informant more official, both for his own safety and in an effort to make himself more available to the police. However, with little experience and no formal training, he felt like a weekend softball player offering services to the major leagues.

"You have other informants in the NGO community helping you in official capacities, right?" Matt asked the policeman, figuring perhaps his help wouldn't even be needed. Surely there were others more qualified to do undercover investigations than a former youth pastor.

"No, you're the only one," came the answer. "We had an Australian, but he left. People like to talk about trafficking, but not a lot of people actually help."

And then the stakes got even higher with the next sentence.

"It would really help if you could wear a hidden camera," the sergeant said. "If you can get evidence on video and give it to us, that is the best for raids and prosecutions."

In a world with a multitude of tip-offs and a lack of witness protection, this request made sense. Covert video evidence of money changing hands documenting children sold for sex was the meat of a strong legal case, the spark to motivate local authorities to kick down the door.

"Do you have a camera I could use?" Matt asked.

"No, our whole team shares one," came the reply from a man obviously expected to work miracles.

❖ ❖ ❖ ❖ ❖

Thanks to Amazon, international shipping, and kids craft supplies, my husband MacGyvered covert surveillance equipment that day. He hid a camera in the inner lining of the backpack and looped a wire through a strap so it disappeared. He created a secret compartment for the battery pack and then hot glued velcro strips to conceal it.

Honestly, I found it hard not to laugh at the whole thing.

My husband had become the only deputized informant with the local government in an entire region of Malaysia, and the police had started handing him tips to pursue on live cases of human trafficking.

And here he was, hot gluing a covert camera we'd purchased off Amazon into an old laptop bag.

What. Was. Happening.

The whole thing was becoming more and more bizarre. A spinning of circumstances I couldn't have imagined when I stood on that stage in familiar Colorado two years ago.

At night, it seemed scary, courageous and epic, but now, as he wielded a miniature hot glue gun, it just felt like *Jason-Bourne-*

Nearly meets *Martha-Stewart-Not-At-All.* The line between stupid and brave, a razor.

Laughable. Humble. Impossible.

"Five loaves and two fish, babe. Five loaves and two fish," was all he said.

Chapter Six

The Line-Up

"O, that's what troubles me, papa. You want me to live so happy, and never have any pain—never suffer anything—not even hear a sad story, when other poor creatures have nothing but pain and sorrow, all their lives.
It seems selfish. I ought to know such things, I ought to feel about them!
Papa, isn't there any way to have all the slaves made free?"
- Harriet Beecher Stowe, *Uncle Tom's Cabin*

"You may choose to look the other way but you can never say again that you did not know."
- William Wilberforce

Eighth Grade North Carolina History branded me. I sat in a desk too small for gangly limbs, and I remember the pervasive gravity that defines most of adolescence—to stand in line and look like everyone else. But then I saw real images from the Atlantic slave trade of the 1800's.

Suddenly, the gravity to behave, to blend in quietly, became a law that should be defied.

Pencil drawings of people like sardines on the lower deck of a slave ship. Dark skinned faces behind literal cages on the shoreline. Bearded white men in large hats and high belts, hands holding a whip or some bills or a drink. African men, women and children with ropes around their feet, perched on blocks— highest bidding for big muscles, large breasts, or healthy teeth. Advertisements with the words, "Good price for healthy Negroes." Bare feet and wide, white eyes.

I remember sitting in that social studies class at 13 years old, and I remember the rage. The tears that I didn't care if even the cool girls saw, the anger as I interrupted the teacher with aggressive questions. Because my people did this. *My* people.

The reality seared, and I remember thinking, "Surely, if I were alive back then, I would have fought this. I would have helped Harriet Tubman. I would have paid for slaves and then let them go free. I would have picketed the auction block or stormed Washington or opened my house to the Underground Railroad. Surely," I claimed inwardly, convicted to my adolescent core, "I would not have stood by and let this happen. If I were alive then, I would have done *something*."

My innate sense of justice needed to believe, *demanded* to believe, that I was not the type of person that could be complicit in the face of loaded ships and auction blocks.

❁ ❁ ❁ ❁ ❁

The moving images looked grainy, jerky. Dark lighting shaded the skin with an eerie glow, and the camera turned crooked at a 45-degree angle. The video feed from Matt's hidden camera looked like something off the *Blair Witch Trials*. Apparently though, the hot glue inside of his computer bag was secure.

My insides felt like spiders, unsure of what I'd see when film rolled further. This was the first actual footage I'd viewed from inside a brothel or bar and some of the first he'd taken, and my anxiety mounted about how I'd react. Flesh and blood strike harder than word and story.

A laptop screen in our bedroom became a virtual window into my husband's previous 12 hours. He had just downloaded the footage and had taken the kids outside to play soccer while I watched it. I heard their squeals through the window, while the image before me of the dark karaoke bar shook in rhythm with the bass of the music blaring there. I saw a karaoke screen on the wall up front, and a machine with microphones sat in the corner.

A young man, early twenties wearing skinny jeans and a smile, brought in a tray of beers. I watched Matt's hand come out from the bottom of the screen and take a bottle.

My husband talked to the server about weather, his age, interests.

"Where are you from?" the young man asked.

In Malay, my husband lied. "I'm from America. I am in the export business. I am here for a month."

A drink entered the screen for just a second. He took a sip, playing the role.

Girls entered. A line of ten. They wore short skirts and high heels. Their long, straight hair, dark and beautiful. They were China dolls with white face powder and long fake lashes.

A mamasan (female pimp) in her young thirties walked in, and I heard her off screen. The camera tipped to the side now, and the 45-degree-angle morphed into 90. I cocked my head to get a better view.

"Which one you like? You can have two," the mamasan said. I knew this initial offer was for karaoke dancing, not sex, though the negotiation for that would come later.

My stomach turned. It felt like a slave block, and I had flashbacks to watching the TV mini-series *Roots* in that eighth grade history class.

The camera straightened as Matt adjusted on the chair. It spun back and forth, capturing girls both confident and tall, awkward and slouched. One tugged at her postage-stamp of a skirt, trying to stretch the material lower. Another had her arms crossed over her lower stomach, pudgy evidence of past motherhood. A third stared blankly straight ahead.

He had about five seconds, maybe ten. And the choice was an important and expensive one. We were using our own income to fuel his investigations, and the roll of cash in his pocket was getting thin.

"Her," I caught the edge of his finger pointing to the right. She was offscreen. "And . . . her." He pointed to the middle—the girl nervously tugging her skirt.

Heads dropped and thin bodies in high heels shuffled out of the room. The ones not chosen. I wondered what went through their minds: "Maybe I'm not pretty enough. Maybe I'm too fat. Maybe no one will love me." And I wondered what public rejection like that did to a girl in a world of selling desirability. Wondered how I would respond on an auction block, passed over and sent away.

Again and again.

I fast forwarded through the next hour of footage because it was nothing more than feet and floor. Matt was still pretty green at using the camera. I hit play, though, when the film caught a brief close-up on the girl who called herself Annie—big eyes, smooth skin, and a body that reminded me of an underdeveloped middle-schooler. One hand still worked to stretch her skirt. I listened as she told Matt her story, though now, the camera was shooting the stained ceiling and the top corner of the door.

She didn't know much Malay, so she used broken English to

explain that she just arrived in the city. On a big bus, filled with other girls, she had traveled from Burma through Thailand until finally reaching Malaysia, a country where prostitution itself was technically illegal. She'd found the job on the internet and thought it was a house cleaning one. Now, however, Annie owed the bar owners money for her bus ticket, work visa and rented room. It was a debt bondage scenario, typical for many of the girls walking red-light districts in SouthEast Asia. She'd been at the karaoke bar for three months.

"How old are you?" I heard Matt ask.

"Eighteen," was the quick reply.

I didn't believe her.

"Adakah ini benar benar? Really, is that true?" My husband questioned. Apparently he didn't either.

✿ ✿ ✿ ✿ ✿

The footage was almost over when I hit play again and watched. This time the lens focused on the mamasan. She was back in the room and had eyes that meant business. Odds were she'd survived her fair share of line-ups in years past, too.

"You can have sex with them. Two girls for three hours. You can go wherever you want, to your hotel. It will be fun," she pushed.

"How much?" I heard my husband ask for prices on prostitutes.

And my mind battled shut-down—his voice in my ears, bartering the price of sex.

"600 ringgit. Less than $200 of your dollars, for two. It's a good deal," she answered.

Since he'd already bought drinks for the girls and paid for the karaoke room for the last hour, I knew he didn't have enough in his pocket. This is a cash-only system for security reasons, and he'd already burned through $200 that night alone.

And though I knew that video footage of the actual sale of victims is the strongest evidence an investigator can capture, my wife's heart sighed relief. He'd only done investigations a total of eight nights so far, and I wasn't sure we were ready for the next step.

I couldn't have predicted how far we'd end up eventually.

"Maybe tomorrow," he said. "Will these girls be here tomorrow?"

"Yes, yes," she affirmed. "They'll be here. They'll wait for you."

❊ ❊ ❊ ❊ ❊

The screen went black, and I tasted eighth grade social

studies. The slave ship from the pictures had become a bus from reality. The auction block with half-naked Africans had morphed into a line-up of barely dressed prostitutes.

This *was* still happening. And it wasn't 12 million this time; it was *27* million.

And this *was* my generation, under my watch.

The gravity to behave and remain unmoved continued to loosen its grip.

Chapter Seven

Fresh Meat

"We believe that in this century the paramount moral challenge
will be the struggle for gender equality
around the world."
- Nicholas D. Kristof and Sheryl WuDunn, *Half the Sky*

"Every time we liberate a woman, we liberate a man."
- Margaret Mead

The guidebooks advised not to bring strollers to rural
Malaysia since the uneven, dirty, or nonexistent sidewalks
rendered wheels ineffective. So, we lifted our preschooler over
potholes in the sidewalk thankful we weren't lugging a heavy
stroller, too. The smell of burning trash and barbecuing pork
mixed with traffic fumes. We walked downtown with three
eager kids to our favorite breakfast place—an outside cafe
grabbing tourists, not locals, with their promise of eggs and
avocado.

Eleven in the morning, and this part of the city was just
waking up. Sleepy tourists, nursing hangovers and unshowered
hair, lounged over coffees as we passed. An anomaly, our family

with three blonde children, walked through a morning world of hippies and backpacks, European men with their potbellies.

Matt led in front with our athletic, easy-going son, Owen. I trailed behind with the girls, one on each side. A block or two left, and a sweaty, sticky heat weighed heavy. I wished I had put the girls in close-toed shoes instead of flip-flops because *goodlord* I'd seen enough rats down here.

From the right came a high-pitched voice and a laugh, "*Sangat Sangat Kacak*. Very, very handsome." Two Malaysian women in their twenties, tank tops and heels, directed attention our way. They stood in front of a bar that got crowded and loud every night after 9, but now stood empty save for themselves and an older, wrinkled woman wiping the counter. The young women assumed we were tourists and didn't speak enough Malay to understand their comments.

They stared at this specimen that was my husband as he walked past.

Fresh meat.

His attractive appearance, Western heritage, young age, and the probable cash lining his pocket made him a walking prize, a trophy.

I was beginning to see the bigger picture of the lives of young women in this country, and it was a difficult reality with which to grapple. I'd spent the last months peering briefly into their worlds, and I knew that they, like our own little family, were largely products of their environments.

Because to a South East Asian woman, especially those born into poor families with little opportunity for education, chances for a stable job are miniscule. With the pressure to provide basics for themselves and financial help for their families, many move into cities in hopes of finding work beyond the basic farming their villages offer. When the girls arrive, disenchantment quickly follows. Jobs are scarce, living expenses high, and the cultural expectation for them to send money to their families is even higher. Many young women fall into prostitution as a means to earn a paycheck.

Extreme poverty leads to extreme decisions. And history has proven prostitution as a potentially lucrative business.

But a handsome "rich" American man like my husband? He can represent for some hard-working women the golden ticket — security, survival, a means to put food on the table and provide fees to send children to school.

I got it. As much as I could.

And while I cringed to have other women openly desiring the only man I'd ever kissed, I cringed even more at the world they were born into — a world where preservation must often be valued above love or romance.

I caught their eyes and smiled, trying to look past my natural tendency to stake my claim. Compassion wasn't strong enough, however, to restrain all the claws.

"*Ya yang benar. Dia adalah sangat kacak,*" I commented to surprised eyes as I walked past. "Yes, that is true. He is *very* handsome."

"What'd those girls say, mom?" Tess asked, a few steps later.

"Oh, they were just talking about how pretty our family was," I answered, mostly telling the truth.

❈ ❈ ❈ ❈ ❈

Ten minutes later, we sat at the cafe enjoying apple-cinnamon waffles, egg burritos, and fruit smoothies, kids sticky and chatty. I disagreed with Matt about what we should get my parents for Christmas, and we talked about plans to visit family next summer during school break. He pulled out his wallet and paid the bill in ringgit, and I fought the guilt that this meal would have fed villagers for a week. He told me I was beautiful, like he did everyday.

We walked back to our car, dodging potholes, trash bags, and the motorcycle that cut an unsuspecting corner. He strode up front again, leading, holding hands with our oldest daughter, a girl who dreamed in princesses and wild horses.

We walked back past the same bar. This time, it stood empty.

Chapter Eight

Through the Lens

"Experience, that most brutal of teachers, but you learn.
My God, do you learn."
- C.S. Lewis

"Let us not be surprised when we have to face difficulties.
When the wind blows hard on a tree, the roots stretch and
grow the stronger. Let it be so with us."
- Amy Carmichael

The next five months became a film reel of covert footage,
spinning always behind closed doors so the kids wouldn't see.

A thousand images clicked by in warp speed, faster than my
heart could absorb. And though I prayed to stay soft—fertile soil
for the injustices of others' stories—I still felt the inevitable
hardening.

Earth can only take so much rainfall after all, until water
bounces off the surface, pools, and runs somewhere else.

❉ ❉ ❉ ❉ ❉

I'd committed to entering the fullness of walking this path with Matt, and we'd agreed that connection and accountability meant I needed to watch the evidence he gathered. And, so, I'd steal away to my bed, lock the door, and open the laptop several times a week.

It felt like visiting the doctor—a dreaded but necessary process.

One video clip followed another, from cities all around SouthEast Asia.

❉ ❉ ❉ ❉ ❉

I saw a European man across the bar, nearly 300 pounds. He wore a sloppy shirt with a small hole in the collar. An empty whisky glass touched sides with a full one in front of him, and he draped his arm casually over the red-lipped, laughing girl beside him. She looked 16, and I doubted if she weighed more than 110 pounds.

In a city in Cambodia, I scanned the fishbowl bar and the pimp that ran it. A line of girls, seated on barstools behind a wall of glass windows. Numbers on their shoulders made it easier for foreign men to choose their dates for the evening. I watched my husband talk of food and travel with the brothel owner—a man I knew was selling innocence for a hefty cut. They laughed over beers like old friends, as the pimp talked about his own daughters back at home and how they adored Justin Bieber.

In Thailand, I watched a conversation with a prostitute under the flashing lights of a large and thriving red-light district. She texted on her iPhone with fingers that flashed with rings when Matt approached her. I listened to the conversation unfold —how she'd worked here for four years, how she liked the hours and the money, how she made enough to send her siblings to school. When Matt asked if she'd ever consider leaving the business, the answer was a fast and committed, "No."

I watched a teenage girl up on a flashy stage dance topless for the first time. She tried to cover herself, arms across chest, embarrassment coloring her face. Offstage the mamasan yelled a threat I didn't understand. The girls on either side stepped in front of her, a shield of seasoned flesh to cover the inexperienced, an act of incredible kindness, on a stripper's stage.

From the virtual vantage point of an attractive white male, I saw the jarring walk down one of the most hedonistic red-light districts in the world. I saw transvestites grab Matt's arm, pulling him towards doors with black curtains. Girls danced in windows on the second floor, and calls came from 360 directions, "Handsome man, you come here! Sex-y!" I saw the waves of flesh and color and humanity brush him from all sides.

I watched from chest-view as he walked into the ground level lobby of a popular hotel, known by underground intel for selling Russian girls. He was told to wait his turn and was then led by a bouncer to the sixth floor. I heard Matt's conversation with the young local man riding the elevator with him. "I've saved for five months for this," the twenty year old said, giddy like he was about to ride the newest roller coaster at an amusement park. I thought of the hotels we'd stayed at as a family all over the country, and I knew so many had looked just like this one. Incredulous, I watched Matt walked down the corridor of the sixth floor of that hotel, each door open, European girls waiting on beds. The twenty year old began to shop, though some doors were already closed.

And I saw, with heart in my throat, the first time my husband gathered evidence in a brothel that only offered on-site sex. The footage rolled as Matt captured the changing of money and the shaky ascent up a dark back stairway. The bedroom door clicked shut, and Matt whispered in fast Malay, "I don't want to sleep with you. I will still pay. I just want to talk. I just broke up with my girlfriend." The 16 year old bowed her head immediately, glad relief spilling, palatable even through the screen, *Terima kasih sangat sangat.* "Thank you very, *very* much."

❊ ❊ ❊ ❊ ❊

And with each passing video clip, each new story, I grew more accustomed to the world that spun in the red-light districts I'd avoided my entire life. Naked bodies didn't surprise me and fear no longer consumed me as Matt's scooter lights disappeared around the corner. My back and my heart became a little more accustomed to the strain.

Over time, we fell into a routine of making this type of work, *work.* We'd Skype-chat, and I'd pray until late when he came home, then I'd let him sleep in the following day, shushing the kids downstairs. We debriefed over coffee, even if it was nearly lunch time, and then I'd watch the footage from the night before while he entered field reports into the computer, the experience still fresh in his memory. We learned that he could do one or two nights of surveillance, and then needed two or three days to recover in those early months.

Thankfully, two of Matt's good friends began partnering with him on surveillance, offering accountability and extra eyes on the ground. For me, anxiously watching the clock until I heard his motorbike pull into the driveway, this was a huge gift.

And the earth hardened just a bit. Like a doctor who must become comfortable with death in order to continue with scalpel in hand, we grew a thicker skin. It was a necessary process for survival.

I just hoped it wouldn't lead to a layer of armor impenetrable.

Chapter Nine

Ghosts

"Anything worth doing, *costs*."

"All this pain, I wonder if I'll every find my way?
I wonder if my life could really change, at all?
All this earth, could all that is lost ever be found?
Could a garden come up from this ground, at all?"
- Gungor, "Beautiful Things"

I didn't want him to touch me. Not really.

He smelled like smoke and cheap perfume. Whose perfume was it?

He'd gotten home early that night. The bar he was investigating was closed, and we were out of money to send him into a more expensive one. It was only 11 p.m.

He made advances.

I asked him to take a shower.

I heard the water running. So did my mind. Images of girls

dancing for him. I knew that any one of them would do anything he had ever fantasized. I replayed the covert reel of their bodies, thin and without the stretch marks I couldn't seem to get rid of, young and without the wrinkles that were creeping around my eyes.

How could I have sex with a man consistently playing the part of a pedophile? How could I make love to my husband wondering if he was imagining another body beneath his and not my own?

❊ ❊ ❊ ❊

Four days earlier, I found him crying in the corner.

He had been out on surveillance the night before in a nearby city and he'd told me in the darkness of our room in the early morning hours about a dark-skinned girl on stage who caught his eye as new to the scene, awkward and uncomfortable. He'd asked an older prostitute about the girl, and she'd said, "She just came from the village. This is her first night. We call her Joy."

Matt had waited all evening for a chance to speak with Joy and wanted to let her know about an alternative job program for girls in the city. He knew that the longer prostitutes were in the business of the flesh-trade, the more difficult it was for them to leave it.

But two hours later, young Joy left with her very first

customer—an older Chinese man who hadn't left her side all night.

A treasure had slipped through my husband's fingers, and it was a haunting knowledge.

It was nearly noon when Matt crawled out of bed and downstairs the following morning. He was drinking a morning cup, bleary-eyed.

The kids and I were taking a break from homeschooling, and the latest Katy Perry song blasted from the playlist. My son started karate-kicking, one daughter tried out her hip-hop moves, and the youngest spun wildly. We were all laughing, enjoying the freedom of dancing when you're too young to care if you're good at it.

And then I turned and saw Matt with his head down, elbows on knees, coffee forgotten. Crying. Not teary-eyed, but full-on sobbing. I quickly stopped the music, scuttled kids upstairs with the promise of television, and then knelt in front of his chair.

"Babe, what's going on?" I asked quietly, expecting something to have triggered a memory from the night before.

He looked up, tears still in hazel eyes.

"This was the song they were playing last night when Joy was dancing for the first time," he muttered. "I just can't get her out of my mind. I wish I could have done something. If I could have gotten there sooner. . ."

Something felt broken inside. The branding of Joy into our story was a reality I never would have chosen, a seared image that left its smoldering mark.

And regardless of how many brothels he investigated or the necessary callus we built over time, there still remained these unplanned moments when the scab was ripped off, triggered by a song, an image or a nightmare. The emotional trauma of watching abuse and pretending that everything was fine, the personal disgust of listening to yourself ask for sex with children, the build-up of fear and the subsequent letdown of adrenaline, these were burdens Matt shouldered alone and try as I might, I knew there were pieces of him in this journey I'd never fully know.

❁ ❁ ❁ ❁ ❁

My husband showered and shaved and climbed into bed. It was past midnight. The ghosts were all there. Joy and Mahi and Annie—the long legs on stage, the seductive calls from the street corner. My own ghosts showed up, too, that night—creeping insecurities, doubt that he still found me beautiful. They whispered and distracted mind and soul, though body was already in motion.

And I can't say they left that night completely, those ghosts, pray and focus as I might. I wish I could say they stay away still.

But that would be a lie.

Sometimes ghosts stick around a while. Good news is, they're pretty thin. They have much less substance than the real flesh and blood right in your bed.

Chapter Ten

Heroes Rising

"Into the streets, we're coming down
We never sleep, Never get tired
Through urban fields, and suburban life

Turn the crowd up now, We'll never back down
Shoot down a skyline, Watch it in primetime
Turn up the love now, listen up now, turn up the love

Who's gonna save the world tonight?
Who's gonna bring you back to life?
We're gonna make it, you and I
We're gonna Save The World tonight

We're far from home, it's for the better
What we dream, it's all that matters
We're on our way, united."

- Swedish Mafia House,
"Who's Gonna Save the World?"

"Play UNO when he gets here," I instructed the kids, "just don't interrupt." Another sweaty day in the tropics, and I'd gone to the cafe in the heart of Kota Baharu armed with activities to distract the children—coloring books, cards, games. Low benches and a small fountain stood beside the deck where we'd grabbed two tables and iced coffees in the corner. We needed somewhere private to talk about a current case and had opted for an isolated spot outside.

"There he is," Matt said, as a tall man with short dark hair named Mike walked towards us. I was a bit intimidated at first, both by the stories I knew about him and his demeanor — military through and through. Matt met him and his partner a few months earlier in a different city and had conducted several investigations with them. Mike had investigated locked brothels, had seen the worst of the worst, and still refused a salary for his efforts. Mike and his team had been involved in key evidence-gathering before, but the realities of the work made them paranoid, and rightly so. They switched hotels, aliases, and cover stories often.

It was one of my first meetings with another undercover operative in real-life. And I was surprised at how easy it was.

He shook my hand and called me "ma'am" with a drawl that reminded me of my own Southern roots. He talked to my kids and asked their names. He chatted about the best places to eat around town.

I felt a bit like I was in the presence of a hero. A hero that had risen in the dark.

Honestly, I was.

＊＊＊＊＊

Over the course of about six months, Matt began connecting with other undercover investigators in Malaysia and even across the border in Thailand. He'd met independent ex-military men, nationals who'd previously worked for other Western NGOs, police that were specific to counter-trafficking efforts, other investigators that were off the grid in many ways. He began developing relationships with them—going on missions together, sharing intel and networks.

After feeling incredibly isolated for so long, Matt began to see there was, indeed, an underground network of qualified investigators operating throughout the country fighting sexual slavery. Over time, Matt worked with 15 different men, living in various corners of Malaysia.

He observed an extreme lack of trust or working partnerships among those active in interventions. In a world of police tip-offs and changing aliases, it wasn't hard to see why. This fragmentation and suspicion, however, led to isolation and ineffectiveness, as oftentimes teams worked the same undercover cases without realizing it.

In addition, Matt saw that most active investigators severely lacked both the funding and equipment to effectively gather the evidence needed for legal raids. Nationals and Westerners alike typically didn't have the networks needed to raise funds to fuel cases and were oftentimes silenced from asking because of the safety risks of working undercover. Those willing to bravely go into dark places for the sake of children were woefully under-equipped and underfunded.

Eventually, the idea of a coalition began to take shape in Matt's mind. He wanted to create a neutral space where quality investigators could work together for the sake of rescue, instead of in competition or isolation. He saw the need for an umbrella organization that could provide benefits, funding, and equipment to investigators, without asking them to sacrifice their safety or even their identities as unique organizations.

My visionary husband wanted to create a coalition not among the talkers, but among the doers, empowering those already knee-deep in intervention, men like Mike and his team.

Matt started calling the fledgling idea The Exodus Road, a path to leave slavery and bondage. But honestly, neither of us was sure it would take.

***

At the cafe table, I handed over the phone to my son to play games, "Here, take turns." UNO had lost entertainment value about 20 minutes ago. I sipped the cold coffee as I listened to Matt and Mike talk about a recent case. Mike was testing a new covert camera we'd just ordered from the States, and they discussed its operating details—low-lighting capabilities, memory cards, and battery life. Mike was one of the first to officially join The Exodus Road coalition, and the two men brainstormed the resources Mike's team needed to successfully work more cases in the future.

Another ten minutes, and the meeting was over. We collected our things.

I turned to shake Mike's hand, and I told him words that he seldom, if ever heard.

"Thank you."

I thanked him for the ways he bravely goes looking for abused children, despite the dangers, and I thanked him for the sacrifices he's made and continues to make. The bumpy bus rides into the jungle. The late nights in smoky bars. The long hours in a dark-windowed car staking out pedophiles. The days away from the comfort of home. The first- person interactions with girls too young to wear makeup and bikinis in brothels.

He shrugged and nodded. Humble.

"We're behind you, Mike. We are. Your work for children, it matters."

I watched Mike pull out of the parking lot on his motorcycle, this man who hailed from such a vastly contrasting world from my own. He was a former special forces officer, I a homeschooling mom. Mike fired weapons and trained in tactical operations; I changed diapers and taught manners. Our differences far outweighed our similarities.

But somehow, I felt connected still the same. A common cause, a shared fight can do that, I supposed.

Maybe this coalition had a shot.

Chapter Eleven

Rescue is Coming

"Please rescue me."
- "Sarah," a trafficked victim who wrote the above
plea on a dollar bill and handed it
to an undercover investigator

"A small body of determined spirits fired by an
unquenchable faith in their mission can
alter the course of history."
- Mahatma Gandhi

Several months into undercover investigations with the Malaysian police, the sergeant came to Matt and asked him to befriend a group of European pedophiles living in Kota Baharu. Six retired men paid for young boys from nearby villages to attend monthly sex parties at their shared compound in the city. The police had photos of the perpetrators and testimony from the neighborhood guard about the activities. But, they couldn't determine which villages the young boys were coming from or who was delivering them—key evidence for the case.

The sergeant drove Matt one afternoon through the suburb of the pedophiles. Their compound was located in an unassuming community, literally five minutes from our house—where our own children rode bikes and played soccer in the front yard.

This case hit close to home. Literally.

The pedophiles went golfing every Wednesday afternoon, and the sergeant asked Matt to join them. He wanted Matt to befriend them, earn their trust, go to one of their parties—all in an effort to gather hard evidence from the inner circle.

And for the first time when presented with a case, Matt said "No." He didn't fit the profile (the men were all significantly older and were European), and he didn't think he could pose convincingly as a pedophile at that level. More than that, our own children were geographically so close, we weren't willing to risk their safety. We shared a local market with this group of · men, after all.

Prone to fighting for solutions, Matt's mind raced through other options immediately. He flipped through his memory rolodex of *CSI* episodes and *James Bond* films.

"Could you gps track their car?" he asked the sergeant.

"We tried," was the answer. "But the battery life only lasts for three days."

In an age of technology, surely there were other tools available.

But Matt left the meeting that day, with no ready answers, just heavy and sick for the young boys delivered like food to the doorstep of hungry men.

❈ ❈ ❈ ❈ ❈

I pulled myself up out of the water of the local pool. I toweled off beneath palm trees swaying against a dull blue sky.

Ding. I dug through a large canvas bag past sunscreen bottles, dive sticks and a broken pair of sunglasses until my fingers found my phone.

Matt: Here now. Minor. Trafficked from Burma. She looks really scared.

I glanced up from the text and saw another ninth grader, worlds away from the one my husband was seeing. The brunette teenager squealed as a friend pushed her into the lukewarm water of the swimming pool, just minutes from our house. I had escaped there with the kids for the evening. Single-parents, even temporary ones, need their outlets.

Ding.

Matt: They call her Sarah. Pray for her. Adil is buying her now.

Water dripped on my arm, as my youngest leaned in. "Can we buy ice cream? *Please?*" she asked. I was a pushover for snacks at any pool, and the kids smelled weakness every time.

Three minutes later, I handed bills across a counter, purchased two chocolates and a vanilla.

I couldn't help but think about the bills handed over in a different part of the country, at the same moment, for an entirely different purpose.

❖ ❖ ❖ ❖ ❖

Three days later, I watched the footage from quiet of my room just after I put the kids to bed. It was the hardest I'd seen yet.

The vantage point was dark as Matt and a lead investigator named Adil, a national with a track record of 300 victim rescues, entered a brothel in a seedy town on the northern tip of the country. They were working a different case whose lead had gone cold, but Adil, the lead investigator, got a break—a call from a pimp.

"We have a fresh girl for you if you want to come in tonight."

Fresh was the word for young. The investigator had spent an entire year developing a relationship with this particular pimp, earning him first dibs on something highly illegal, someone "fresh."

On my computer screen, I watched the girls walk in behind the glass windows. It was another fishbowl bar, and the stools were already lined up for the prostitutes. Dressed like so many others I'd seen via the hidden portal of the covert camera, the girls wore high heels, short dresses, sprayed hair, heavy makeup. They walked in, perched themselves on the stools. Some looked at cell phones, others talked to the girl beside them.

The pimp lounged across from Matt, and I saw the right side of the other investigator sitting on the couch. Adil led the conversation and told a story that made the pimp laugh. They ordered a beer and then the pimp, a boisterous man with a wide face and wider belly, motioned for someone in the back shadows.

"*Datang.* Come," he commanded with authority.

And Sarah shuffled toward the couch.

She was dressed in street clothes, disheveled hair. Her eyes never left the floor, and she fiddled with a napkin, tearing it into little shreds.

I watched as men talked over her, laughed around her. Sarah had been sold by her mother in Burma, trafficked across Thailand and now into Malaysia, and had landed here—in a brothel, without money or passports, unable to speak the local language.

Two days earlier, they sold her virginity for $600.

She was 15 years old.

I watched the choppy footage of Sarah and her shredded napkin, and I couldn't breathe. Anger welled in me, helplessness, the injustice nearly suffocating.

The price was bartered at $300—expensive because this would only be Sarah's third sexual encounter. The transaction was recorded on covert film, money changed hands. And I watched as Adil led Sarah up a dark stairway, and out of my sight.

✿ ✿ ✿ ✿ ✿

The video file ended, but Matt told me the rest of the details later that night. Adil closed the door in Sarah's brothel and phoned a social worker fluent in Burmese. The social worker asked questions, heard Sarah's story of slavery, and explained that Adil might be able to help.

The investigator left an hour later with a promise to return and with a dollar bill in his possession. On the bill, an unexpected message.

Sarah had scrawled on the only piece of paper in the room, "Please rescue me," in shaky Burmese script.

It was a brave cry for freedom, carried out of a brothel, in the pocket of a pair of jeans.

❖ ❖ ❖ ❖ ❖

Young boys delivered to pedophiles, the virginity of teenagers sold for a premium, these were the realities that became threads in the fabric of our lives, woven into our everyday. And the more the stories came to light, the more resolved we became to invade the dark.

Rescue needed to be more than a trendy, dramatic word. It needed to become a reality.

Chapter Twelve

Riverside

"It is not the critic who counts; not the man who points out
how the strong man stumbles, or where the doer of deeds
could have done them better.

The credit belongs to the man who is actually in the arena,
whose face is marred by dust and sweat and blood; who
strives valiantly . . . who spends himself in a worthy cause;

who at the best knows in the end the
triumph of high achievement,
and who at the worst, if he fails, at least fails while daring
greatly, so that his place shall never be with those cold and
timid souls who neither know victory nor defeat."

- Theodore Roosevelt

"Looks like two of the three things are arising," Matt told me
as he used sticky rice as a spoon and grabbed a dripping handful
of som tam—spicy papaya salad, a local staple.

The river rushed beside the bamboo stilted platform on
which we sat. My three white children played with a dozen
caramel-skinned ones, set apart once again. I glanced around the

banks of the river, and noticed most eyes were also fixated where mine were—on blonde heads and the children born with them. I felt like we were all a bit like circus animals.

The kids hugged inner tubes, and I was thankful they didn't notice they had drawn an audience, thankful the other children in the water raced with them down a small rapid between the rocks. Children tend to see beyond skin and hair more quickly than adults.

I wanted to freeze the moment once more because I had a sinking feeling we wouldn't be back here again, to this waterfall with its cafes and bamboo structures. I had a dread that my lips wouldn't burn from the chilies in the som tam after this summer, that my hands wouldn't drive a scooter with three children behind me, that my tongue would grow even slower with the local language I'd worked so hard to understand. I had a suspicion that our chapter was closing overseas, and there were moments, like this one, that I desperately didn't want to leave Malaysia.

Restaurants catered to the huts dotting the riverside where small groups of families or friends circled around a shared meal. Ours felt a bit lonely with just Matt and I.

"I mean, when you think about it, they are much more qualified than I am—all of them, " he said, taking huge gulps from the glass bottle of Fanta— he'd asked the waitress for the som tam to be hot. She'd listened, and his mouth was on fire.

I knew he was right. The other investigators were more qualified.

The Exodus Road coalition had slowly gathered a bit of traction over the past months, and the investigators and organizations interested in joining it came with much higher credentials in the investigative realm than my husband.

As we talked and processed, we saw three necessary roles to launch this idea of a coalition that empowers rescue for the modern-day sex slave. We needed undercover investigators, a field director who already had established relationships with local authorities, and a storyteller to raise funding and spearhead efforts in the United States.

I rolled the sticky rice in my fingers as my feet dangled over the water. I dipped a corner of it into the spicy-sweet chili sauce that had become to me like ketchup was to my children.

We had connections with 15 undercover investigators at the time. They were all experienced, quality men.

Two days earlier, we had also just learned one of Matt's close friends, with an excellent mind and strong relationships with the local police, had agreed to be our field director to manage cases and finances for The Exodus Road from Kota Baharu itself.

This left only one of the three roles still vacant—the storyteller, located back home in the United States.

While Matt could do investigations, and while he had the

skills to do case management, we both knew life experience had hammered him into an inspirational leader and motivational communicator over the last ten years. We understood that with his firsthand experience of sexual slavery and personal relationships with the men on the ground, he would have the tools he needed to communicate authentically, to be the voice and ask for resources when brave men couldn't go public themselves.

The next step became clear: the best way we could serve the field was to leave it.

❖ ❖ ❖ ❖ ❖

My mind drifted like the quickly-moving current at my feet. I thought about Sarah, still hidden in a dirty room somewhere, waiting for rescue. I wondered what she was thinking in that moment. Surely, she couldn't know the army of forces mobilizing with her in mind. I knew she couldn't understand that Adil was taking the case to high officials in the capital, was presenting evidence, was organizing a swat team. I knew she didn't realize the NGO community was rallying, and that we personally were giving money to fuel rescue efforts. She only had the hope of a promise from a man she didn't know. I wondered if she was scared. Or hurt.

I wondered how many times she had been used.

My son Owen, the adventurer, was precariously on his knees

on the inner tube. The water pulled him forcefully down the rapid, around a rock, and into the circulating pool below. Lilly was independently digging by the riverbank, while Tess was chatting dynamically with the Malaysian storekeeper who rented the tubes to us. I wondered how far her Malay could take her in the conversation.

I worried about the scars these three would carry from this place, the things from which we hadn't been able to shield them. I wondered if they'd carry ghosts, too, years from now, when ketchup was at every table and English on every tongue.

The fragrance of orchids met me, and I looked across the table at my husband. His wrinkles were deeper than they were three years ago, his words and soul deeper still. My high school prom date carried the weight of many worlds during our time overseas, from holding our family together at home to holding a teenager's hand in a brothel. Malaysia branded him, rescue had cost him, and real victims would forever live in his memories.

But somehow he had emerged stronger from it all. And I admired him even more.

The waitress plodded down the uneven steps and asked if we needed anything else. We told her no, and I motioned the kids to start heading in.

Our time was coming to a close.

I finished the last of the som tam, sticky rice in hand, and I thought about loaves and fish there by the riverside that day. I wondered if our small offerings on Asian soil could ever be multiplied like the disciples' was.

And the kids pulled themselves out and toweled off—full-hearted, but so very tired.

Immersion in a raging river will do that to a soul.

The End.

The Story Continues
The Exodus Road

"Never doubt that a small group of thoughtful, committed
citizens can change the world; indeed, it's the
only thing that ever has."
- Margaret Mead

The story of The Exodus Road continues today in ways
we never could have predicted when we boarded a plane in July
2012, bound this time for North America. The following are
several brief snapshots of The Exodus Road coalition's evolution
to include more organizations and support more rescues than
expected over the course of its first year of existence.

Sarah

Sarah's story didn't end in a brothel. The 15 year old
victim who wrote, "Please rescue me," on a bill and handed it, in
wild hope, to an undercover investigator, is no longer sold for
sex. Sarah is free.

Adil, the national investigator, pushed Sarah's case to
authorities over the course of two long months. Initial attempts
to rescue Sarah failed due to corruption. When the first swat
team assembled, the raid location was leaked. Brothel owners
hid Sarah and the other underage victims enslaved in that
establishment. But Adil would not relent. He stationed his team

covertly in the city for an entire month, watching and waiting for Sarah to be put back into play in the brothel.

Finally, young Sarah was up for sale again. A united effort from the NGO community and the local and national police joined once again to raid Sarah's brothel.

Five minutes before the swat teams ascended, the unthinkable. Detailed information about the raid was again leaked by a different informant. Sarah could not be found in the brothel. Adil, however, would not be stopped. He raced through a local market, spotted other girls he recognized from the same brothel and followed them. A frantic phone call later, and young Sarah literally ran from the house and jumped into Adil's waiting car at the gate. The raid was then triggered, and seven other underage victims were rescued.

It was like something out of an action film. But it wasn't a Hollywood script; this was real life. And while we understood that most cases likely wouldn't include blockbuster endings, Adil's tenacity for justice in his own country inspired us to keep moving forward.

Pedophiles

Matt couldn't stop thinking about the pedophile case the sergeant asked him to cover, and though the original intel on the gps tracking unit needed to bust the older men was a battery life of three days, internet research led Matt to find a unit that was motion activated, providing a battery life of up to six months. A church in the US bought the device, and Matt delivered it just days before we left Malaysia.

A few weeks later, the tracking unit was covertly placed

on the underside of the truck of the suspected trafficker. And while the driver was in the process of picking up and delivering two village boys to pedophiles in the city, his car became a moving *blip* on the screen of the police sergeant. A sting operation underway, the young boys stepped out of the truck, and the swat team ascended. The boys were immediately taken to safety, and the pedophile on scene arrested and soon extradited to his home country, to face a public trial.

The fight for the innocence of children had just enlisted modern technology—common in the Western world, but new to the developing one.

And, thankfully, it worked.

Eighty-Nine

May 3, 2013—The pings of texts from India began at 4:30 a.m. With a big raid scheduled for that morning, we weren't sure what the day would bring. Two months earlier, Matt had connected through a mutual friend with a team of national investigators in Mumbai, India. He had spent time with them on the ground, and suddenly the concept for The Exodus Road coalition crept into another country. The team there had requested funds for the raid of a particular dance bar, known for underage prostitution. The bar was three kilometers from the local police station, implying complicity, so the investigators reached out to another police branch to help with the case.

We were back in the States at this point and sent out a call to our community—both online and in real-life. To our surprise, in four days, the funds poured in to empower the raid.

And here we were, breaking news of rescue from the

phone in Matt's hand:

6:00 am: *Raid today. Making plan now with police.*

7:12 am: *Here inside dance bar. Police will trigger raid anytime.*

8:15 am: *Many girls. More than we thought. All are safe.*

9:37 am: *89 girls rescued. 32 minors. All have been trafficked. 42 arrested.*

The team of four local investigators who were the real heroes in this rescue had been working for the past ten years for the justice of women and children in their local community. They shared one covert camera, with broken buttons, and scraped by monthly with a trickle of funding from the West.

Through a grant, The Exodus Road provided the team with over $5,000 worth of covert gear and through individual donations, we helped supply consistent resources for investigations, raids, and even contract salaries.

We began to see that when men like the team in India have the tools they need to be effective in the field, freedom's floodgates open wide.

Wider even, than expected.

(For documented footage of this raid, please you visit the Vimeo channel of The Exodus Road.)

Freedom Rocks

Glass jars filled with common river rocks sit in the entryway of The Exodus Road's stateside office in Colorado today. Each rock bears the name of a victim and the location and date they were rescued out of brothels or sexual slavery. Each rescue was supported—through staffing, equipment, or funding—by The Exodus Road, and each was carried out by the valiant efforts of partners in the field, both in SouthEast Asia and in India. At the time of this writing (August 2013), thirteen months into officially operating as a coalition, the rocks keep multiplying.

Today, there are 191 of them. We call them Freedom Rocks. And they serve to physically remind us that Every. One. Matters.

We're miles away now from that moment when my daughter Lilly brought me the stone by the creek in Malaysia and asked me to see it, to care for it. The journey between the rocks—the single one held in a toddler's hands and the stacks that now sit in our office—has been admittedly a brutal, gritty one. It's been a road I never expected to walk. More often than not, our failures and inadequacies outweighed our victories and competencies.

But here's the thing I am continuing to learn about freedom, about any kind of sacrifice made on behalf of another—it always multiplies.

Maybe there's something to that five loaves and two fish story, after all.

Puzzle Pieces

People ask us often when they hear our story, "So what am I supposed to do now?"

At first, we never really answered in specifics. Because the issue of modern-day slavery is a complex, expanding puzzle that spans the globe and generations, and no one can predict the piece each person has been given to play to fuel freedom.

And this is true. I won't pretend that I know your story or how it relates to mine. I don't know how your life connects to the oppression you've read in these pages. Perhaps it is your own abuse or that of a loved one. Maybe it's a deep sense of justice that rallies when you hear of busloads of victims transported across borders. Perhaps you've heard a story or seen a video that keeps you awake at night, that moves you with a gut-level need to *do something.* There is no formula here, no prescription for what it looks like to become a modern-day abolitionist, a part of today's Underground Railroad, a brick on the Exodus Road.

I used to leave people with a vague sense that they should just keep moving forward, keep engaging with the issue, and that eventually, their next unique puzzle piece would fall into their hands.

But friends, we're on the field with our faces are painted Scottish blue. And William Wallace didn't yell for his men to keep *thinking* about fighting for justice, didn't call them to wait for the answers to come in a convenient time and place.

Because vague doesn't call soldiers from the ridge and onto the battlefield. Waiting doesn't rescue children in brothels.

And so today, when people ask me, "What should I do?" I tell them simply, "You should help rescue slaves." And then I tell them about our Search and Rescue program at The Exodus Road and how we let donors hire one of our undercover investigative teams to go into dark places and look for victims. I let them know that in this monthly gift, they literally empower men like Mike and Adil and the Colonel Sergeant to kick down brothel doors. I tell them about our advocacy programs here where people can fund raids or covert equipment, after-care initiatives or awareness events in their own communities. I let them know about other quality organizations, too, effectively fighting slavery, and I ask them to volunteer to others their time or skills—their puzzle pieces.

I don't tell them to wait for the perfect or simple answer. And neither would Sarah or Mali or Annie or Joy.

Because justice *is* in the hands of the ordinary, and if rescue is going to come on our watch, we need an army of passionate, committed people to bring it.

FAQ

Below we've answered some of the most common inquires we get about The Exodus Road. If you have other questions or would like to know more about current cases, rescues we've supported, or stories from the field, check out our website, www.theExodusRoad.com.

What is The Exodus Road?

The Exodus Road is a coalition of organizations and individuals fighting sex slavery and human trafficking. The coalition exists to facilitate and empower undercover investigations, raids and rescues for victims, and the arrests of criminals—all in close partnership with local governments. The Exodus Road is not a religious organization and works respectfully with people of all faiths and backgrounds.

As of August 2013, we support and are networked with 124 undercover investigators and have directly empowered the rescues of 191 victims of sexual slavery in SE Asia and India. We have delivered over 100 pieces of quality covert equipment to field teams in 12 months, and we maintain two offices—one in Colorado, USA, and the other in SE Asia. We have field directors in SE Asia, India, and the United States.

The two heartbeats of our nonprofit are collaboration and empowerment.

What does The Exodus Road provide for coalition members?

We work to provide operational funding for investigative cases, professional covert equipment, operative support and training, and partnerships within the intervention community. Our goal is to make those already active in field investigations more effective. Every investigator we support is trained, and many are former military or police staff. Our home office in the United States works to provide the resources field teams need. The organizations in our coalition are free to maintain their own autonomy, but must adhere to standard operating procedures of the coalition while on funded missions. By empowering them, we empower rescue.

We set a priority of hiring and fueling national efforts in the field first, understanding that nationals will be the most effective force for change in their own cultures.

Why investigations and prosecutions?

Experts typically break the fight against modern-day slavery into three broad areas: prevention, intervention, and after-care. All three are essential components to bringing freedom to the millions of slaves around the world.

Currently, we promote prevention by educating others and raising awareness on the realities of human trafficking, primarily through social media and video campaigns. Similarly, we support restoration initiatives by financially supporting and networking with qualified after-care and advocacy programs.

The Exodus Road, however, maintains its chief focus on facilitating targeted interventions. We believe a key strategy in slowing the global trafficking machine lies in working within the local legal system to bring justice and accountability. When local police conduct raids and arrests, the sale of slaves becomes a riskier, more expensive (and thus, less desirable), business.

Who are the investigators?

The undercover operatives we support come from a variety of backgrounds. Some are former military or police, others have been trained by NGOs. The investigators represent both nationals and foreigners, but all are qualified investigators with field experience. Most work for other organizations or the local government, run a nonprofit themselves, or simply volunteer their time. Due to security risks, membership in the coalition is anonymous and the identities of the investigators themselves are not revealed unless otherwise requested by the agents.

What about after-care?

After-care is an essential component in any redemptive rescue from sexual slavery. And while The Exodus Road does not claim expertise in holistic after-care, we network with several facilities and organizations who do. When our investigative teams assist in a raid or rescue, we try to immediately place victims into a private after-care facility in our

90

network. Ultimately, however, the authority for victim placement is in the hands of the government, and often victims are placed into government facilities to await interviews or repatriation to their home countries.

We direct a portion of our funding to after-care facilities which receive rescued victims to help cover the expenses of that child's placement and are working diligently to develop and fund better advocacy measures for trafficking survivors.

What can I do?

We can't tell you what your puzzle piece is in this fight for freedom. But, we can say that there are many opportunities to practically get involved and make a real difference. *Today.* Don't let the magnitude of the numbers immobilize you. You can:

- Sponsor an investigator to look for victims trapped in sexual slavery by joining a Search and Rescue team. (www.theExodusRoad.com/search-and-rescue)

- Become an advocate and host a fundraising event to sponsor a raid or purchase a piece of covert gear for a field investigator for The Exodus Road.

- Join the blogging team of writers (#blog4rescue) who use their online spaces to speak for the oppressed.

- Volunteer your skills or talent with The Exodus Road in our volunteer center.

- Get educated and lobby politically for more resources or stronger laws to fight modern-day slavery.

- Connect and share online about rescue and empowerment efforts.

- Investigate other organizations effectively fighting modern day slavery and support their work financially or with volunteer hours.

- Watch covert footage from The Exodus Road field teams on our Youtube or Vimeo channels and share the footage with your networks.

- Research quality after-care facilities and invest in their efforts.

- Buy fair trade to support sustainable lifestyles for vulnerable communities.

The options *do* exist—both with The Exodus Road and within other organizations effectively fighting for freedom. If you'd like to consider empowering our work specifically, check out our website, www.theExodusRoad.com, for information about investing in and connecting with our field teams.

Our Gratitude

We are so grateful to many who walked The Exodus Road with us.

First, we thank our three children, Tess, Owen, and Lilly. We are confident our story, even the difficult parts, will be rich chapters in your own lives. We're hopeful you'll fall in love with Jesus, and we feel confident he'll use your five loaves and two fish in mighty ways in the world.

We are especially grateful for our families, who laid on the altar the sacrifice of *time* on behalf of child rescue. To our dads and moms, we know it hasn't been easy having us as the parents of your grandchildren, but words can't communicate how far you have launched us. Your encouragement has been crucial to us personally and you have loved our family generously despite the distance. And to our siblings and their spouses, Steven, Amy, Cassie, Chad, Michelle, Will, and Shannon, thank you for putting up with Christmases over Skype and relationships via emails. We are grateful you all are more than family we endure; you are friends we enjoy.

We'd like to thank our friends who walked with us overseas. The Stowell, Rathmell, Reynolds, Karum, Wessel, Sagunaniwet, Lindeman, and Nakamura families were all key in our survival and perspective. And to the Stowells, we will forever remember lunches at Favorite Place.

We'd also like to thank all of our friends and faith community who supported us both financially and in prayer throughout our time overseas and who still do today. Your Skypes, emails, financial gifts, and visits spoke hope in dark places. You trusted us and stuck with us when many would have chosen to support an "easier" work. The Exodus Road is your story, your victory, too. Those freedom rocks have your fingerprints on them.

A special thanks goes to Kelley Leigh, without whose encouragement and artful eye, this book would have had many more misplaced commas and description-lacking scenes.

To the stateside staff of The Exodus Road, thank you for bringing your very best to the table for the girl in the back room. We are so deeply thankful to have each of you on the team. Here's to many more sushi-celebratory lunches.

And finally, to all the hard working investigators and advocates in the field who we've had the honor of meeting in person, and to those with whom we have yet to intersect, we remain grateful for your willingness to collaborate for the sake of rescue. You are true heroes and the bravest people we know.

15820132R00061

Made in the USA
San Bernardino, CA
09 October 2014